THE GENEROSITY GAP

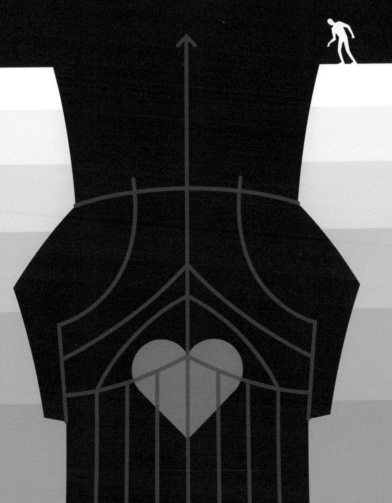

How Christians' Perceptions and Practices of Giving Are Changing—
and What It Means for the Church

A Barna Report Produced in Partnership with Thrivent Financial

CONTENTS

PREFACE

by Christopher J. Kopka

In our organization's efforts to serve and walk alongside the Church, Thrivent Financial recently commissioned Barna Group to perform qualitative and quantitative research around the subject of generosity. We originally thought the research would help us prove or disprove a set of commonly held assumptions and beliefs expressed by pastors toward an entire generation: Millennials.

You'll see that this research report does indeed bust some generational myths. What we and Barna did not anticipate, however, was that the research would yield an even deeper set of insights. How do we collectively understand generosity? And where do we as church leaders or churchgoers have *misunderstandings* about generosity? Is it possible to both know and grow generosity in all its expressions? Might it even be possible to order our daily lives around generosity in ways that demonstrate loving God and loving our neighbors?

We're honored to be a part of this important work with Barna. *The Generosity Gap* provides a snapshot of "what is," not "what should be." Some of the findings are encouraging and hopeful. Others are, well, a bit disappointing. Taken together, however, *The Generosity Gap* provides a realistic look at the state of generosity in the North American church.

What you will *not* find in this monograph is also worth mentioning. You won't find a laundry list of five, eight or 10 "to dos." That does not mean that you shouldn't hammer out your own list of next steps and actions. You should! Yet we, with Barna, feel

Chris Kopka describes himself as a poet by passion, a lawyer by training and a business strategist by accident. His personal mission? Helping people to see themselves as blessed so they might share their blessings. (He also bakes bread.) Chris joined Thrivent Financial in 2006, where he currently serves as President of Church Solutions Group leading Thrivent's church-related business and functions. He and author / painter Anna Dvorak have been married since 2004.

there's something different about this research. It doesn't lend itself to one-size-fits-all solutions to giving. There's no quick fix for the engagement challenges discussed in this report.

Instead, we want churches not only to read *The Generosity Gap* research, but also to *interact* with the data and with one another. Frankly, we are convinced that significant lessons can be learned from this study about fostering generosity and engagement—especially among Millennial Christians.

The Generosity Gap offers readers a remarkable invitation, an invitation to think deeply, to pray boldly, to explore courageously, to question tenaciously and to act fearlessly. In that process—both alone and in conversation with others—we believe churches can spur generosity that grows people's engagement with their faith, not solely supports the church's financial needs.

For more than 100 years, Thrivent Financial—a not-for-profit membership organization of Christians—has sought to help its members be wise with money and live generously. *The Generosity Gap* builds on our mission to grow the wisdom of the Church as a body about how to help all people live generously.

It is our great pleasure to partner with Barna in bringing you *The Generosity Gap*. We trust that it will be a blessing to all readers, and especially to those in church leadership.

For pastors and church leaders ready to learn more about generosity best practices and insights through our soon-to-be completed digital community, I invite you to visit our website at **InsightWise.org**.

Thank you for your decision to read *The Generosity Gap*. May the lessons you learn in the pages of this report be a blessing to you and to others in our shared journey toward generous living!

Christopher J. Kopka
President, Thrivent Church Solutions Group
Fellow Generosity Sojourner

Join our community
at **InsightWise.org**

INTRODUCTION

There are both practical and spiritual reasons for churches and Christian organizations to encourage Christians to live generously. Practically speaking, churches have bills to pay and communities to serve, and Christian nonprofits can't do their good work without adequate financial and volunteer resources. These needs are real and ongoing, and most can only be met with dollars and time donated by consistently generous Christians.

From a spiritual standpoint, generosity according to the Scriptures is, among other things:

- A hallmark of a good life: "The generous will prosper" (Prov. 11:25).

- A natural response to God's generosity: "Everything we have has come from you, and we give you only what you first gave us!" (1 Chron. 29:14)

- A benchmark of our love for God: "I was hungry and you fed me. I was thirsty, and you gave me a drink.... When you did it to one of the least of these my brothers and sisters, you were doing it to me!" (Matt. 25:34–40)

- A principal way to obey Christ: "Share each other's burdens, and in this way obey the law of Christ" (Gal. 6:2).

Most U.S. Christians today do not live up to the biblical ideal. People tend to think of themselves as at least somewhat generous, yet few who intend to give 10 percent of their income actually do so. Forms of generosity other than financial giving are hard to track, but few Christians do as much as they would like in the way of service, kindness, hospitality and similar generous acts. Why? What factors make generosity a challenge for most people? And among those who *are* notably generous with money, time and other resources, what attitudes, practices, expectations or perceptions contribute to their open-handed habits?

CHANGING REALITY, WIDENING GAPS

The need for answers is not theoretical. As the proportion of Christians in the U.S. continues to shrink with each successive generation,* the base of givers and volunteers on whom churches and Christian nonprofits depend is also shrinking. Practicing Christians—who say their faith is very important in their life and have attended a worship service within the past month—are a diminishing slice of the overall population. In 2001, 45 percent of all U.S. adults qualified as practicing Christians. In 2017, just 34 percent meet the criteria. And among Millennials, the youngest adults, the proportion is even smaller: Just one in five is a practicing Christian (21%).

Not only are Millennials less likely to practice Christianity and, thus, to financially support a local church; they also have less money to spend on such support. According to a report released by investment giant Morgan Stanley, "Millennials have grown up in the shadow of the Great Recession, are saddled with higher education debt and housing costs, and are forming households later. These facts dramatically affect how Millennials spend."[1] Additionally, they face a tougher job market than when previous generations were starting their careers. In 1990, 77 percent of 20– to 34-year-olds were employed. By 2012, the percentage had dropped to 67 percent—a massive decline whose effects are still

> Few Christians do as much as they would like in terms of service, kindness and hospitality. Why?

*Millennials (born 1984 to 2002), Gen-Xers (born 1965 to 1983), Boomers (born 1946 to 1964) and Elders (born 1945 or before).

being felt half a decade later. It wasn't until 2015 that Millennial employment once again crept over 70 percent, where it continues to hover today.[2]

On top of these factors, the overall employment landscape has changed dramatically. According to *Forbes* there are 53 million freelancers in America today, and it's estimated that one out of every two workers will be a freelancer by 2020.[3] That means a "steady paycheck" isn't necessarily all that steady, even for those who work 40 or more hours a week. As you can see in the table, few people donate, or tithe, 10 percent or more of their income—but even if more of them did, the dollar amount of their donations would likely be less consistent than in decades past, when work was more consistent.

PERCENTAGE OF U.S. ADULTS WHO REPORT DONATING 10 PERCENT OR MORE OF INCOME, BY GENERATION

	% Millennials	% Gen-Xers	% Boomers	% Elders
To a church	1	2	3	7
To a nonprofit	3	4	5	8
Did not tithe to a church or nonprofit	95	93	92	85

July 2016, *n*=1,556 U.S. interested Christians.

But financial giving is not the only way of living generously, nor the only method under strain. Rather than working eight hours and heading home, more people than ever, thanks to networked technology, are "always on" and always "on call." Their available time for volunteering, hospitality and making connections with others is shrinking alongside boundaries between work and life.

All these factors (and others) are creating immense "gaps" in Christian generosity and making urgent the case for us to rethink churches' efforts.

MAKING A STUDY OF GENEROSITY

If the groups they lead are to survive and adapt to this changing reality, pastors and organizational leaders need both accurate information and wisdom for applying data to their particular context. Commissioned by Thrivent Financial, Barna researchers designed a study to assess Christians' perceptions and habits of generosity. Our hope for *The Generosity Gap* is to provide the data and insights leaders need to help each other navigate the years ahead.

Researchers designed a three-phase study. First, Barna conducted qualitative interviews with U.S. adults ages 18 to 69. Some, but not all, of these adults identified as Christians. As part of the qualitative phase, researchers also interviewed Protestant pastors through Barna's PastorPanel. Insights gleaned from open-ended interviews in the qualitative phase guided researchers' design of the survey instruments used in nationwide polling.

Second, the Barna team designed a quantitative survey for self-identified Christians. The questionnaire included several screening questions so that insights derived from the study would be maximally useful to pastors and ministries that work primarily through churches: Self-identified Christians who report they have *never* attended church and who *disagree* that their faith is important for their lives were screened out of participation. Those included in the final sample could be called "interested Christians," since they indicate that faith is or might be important to them, and either currently attend or have been involved in a church at some point in their lives. To avoid needless complexity, "interested Christians" are most often referred to in this report just as "Christians."

Third, researchers designed a quantitative survey for U.S. Protestant pastors. Many of the questions parallel those from the survey of Christians, so that analysis can reveal similarities and differences between church leaders and interested Christians.

And, indeed, there are differences—"generosity gaps"—to be found between pastors and Christians, between Christians of

> There are generosity gaps between pastors and Christians, between Christians of different generations, and between people's intentions and habits

different generations, and between people's intentions and habits. To make these accessible, we've structured our analysis around Jesus' command to "love the LORD your God with all your heart, all your soul, all your mind, and all your strength" (Mark 12:30).

- **The Mind Gap:** Pastors' views on how people ought to express generosity are different from other Christians'. *How can leaders teach more clearly on how to think about Christian giving?*

- **The Heart Gap:** Different generations tend to think differently about generosity and act generously in diverse ways. *How can leaders help Christians of different ages acknowledge their differences and reconcile with one another?*

- **The Soul Gap:** Christians with "giving" goals give more, while those with "keeping" goals give less. *How can leaders help people orient their life's purpose toward God and others, rather than themselves?*

- **The Strength Gap:** Churchgoers who consider generosity important are not always aware of their opportunities to give. *How can leaders help people turn their desire to give into regular habits, especially with the help of technology?*

The Generosity Gap explores each of these and offers leaders a starting point for generating solutions. Our prayer is that pastors and other Christian leaders will use these data to help each other strategize for the future, dreaming up fresh tactics for how to connect Christians' heart, mind and soul with their potential strength of generosity.

Time & Money

Volunteer hours and donor dollars are bread and butter for churches and nonprofits.
Here's a breakdown of who is most likely to give one or the other (or both).

Different generations have different priorities when it comes to generosity. But what does that mean in practice, when it comes to sacrificing their time and financial resources?

Millennials

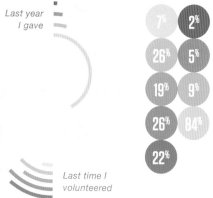

Last year I gave

7% 2%
26% 5%
19% 9%
26% 84%
22%

Last time I volunteered

Gen-Xers

Last year I gave

8% 15%
27% 24%
19% 18%
25% 43%
21%

Last time I volunteered

Boomers

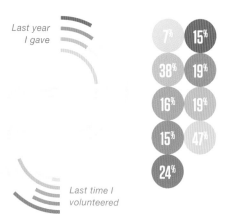

Last year I gave

7% 15%
38% 19%
16% 19%
15% 47%
24%

Last time I volunteered

Elders

Last year I gave

4% 25%
27% 18%
18% 20%
12% 37%
39%

Last time I volunteered

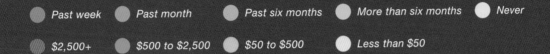

Past week **Past month** **Past six months** **More than six months** **Never**

$2,500+ **$500 to $2,500** **$50 to $500** **Less than $50**

It turns out that giving time and giving money go hand in hand. Those who give more money volunteer more often. And those who volunteer more often give more money.

Last Time I Volunteered, by How Much I Gave

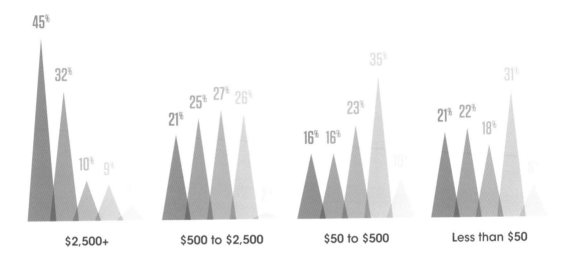

| $2,500+ | $500 to $2,500 | $50 to $500 | Less than $50 |

45% 32% 10% 9% | 21% 25% 27% 26% | 16% 16% 23% 35% 10% | 21% 22% 18% 31%

How Much I Gave, by the Last Time I Volunteered

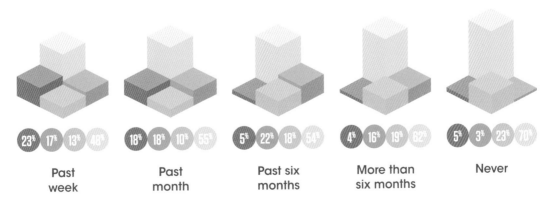

Past week 23% 17% 13% 48%

Past month 18% 18% 10% 55%

Past six months 5% 22% 18% 54%

More than six months 4% 16% 19% 62%

Never 5% 3% 23% 70%

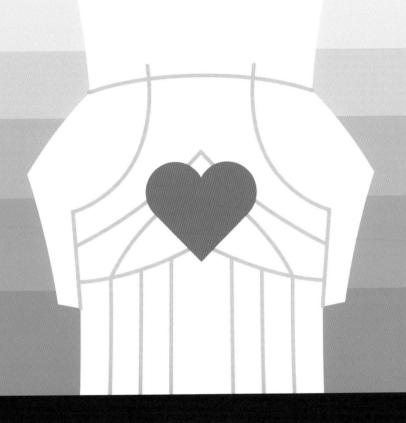

THE GENEROSITY GAP

1.THE MIND GAP

KEY FINDINGS

- Pastors tend to believe generosity is a matter of planning, discipline and sacrifice, while many younger Christians think spontaneity and compassion are essential to generosity.
- Christians whose parents were generous during their childhood are more likely to highly value generosity as adults.
- Pastors talk about serving more than they talk about giving—with unintended consequences.
- The people who are most likely to serve or volunteer also tend to give most financially.

As a rule, Christians and pastors have similar, but not identical, ideas about what characteristics make an act generous, or not. In general, most agree that generosity comes from an unselfish, sincere spirit, not from a sense of obligation or of self-interest. Compared with Christians, a larger percentage of pastors agree that generosity is *always* "a response to Christ's love" (66% vs. 47% all Christian adults). Church leaders are also more likely to believe generosity is both an inward attitude and an outward discipline, and are less likely than Christians generally to say it has to do with either spontaneity or a sense of duty.

On the other hand, Christians are more likely than pastors to say generosity is *always* spur-of-the-moment and a result of compassion—beliefs that may indicate some romanticism attached to the notion of generosity. They are also more likely to say it is *never* or *seldom* "sacrificial" (16% vs. 5% pastors).

GENEROSITY IS "ALWAYS"

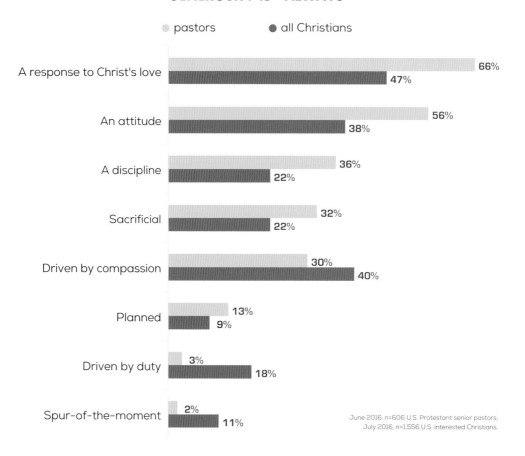

○ pastors   ● all Christians

	pastors	all Christians
A response to Christ's love	66%	47%
An attitude	56%	38%
A discipline	36%	22%
Sacrificial	32%	22%
Driven by compassion	30%	40%
Planned	13%	9%
Driven by duty	3%	18%
Spur-of-the-moment	2%	11%

June 2016, *n*=606 U.S. Protestant senior pastors;
July 2016, *n*=1,556 U.S. interested Christians.

When it comes to generations, younger Christians are more likely than older adults to perceive generosity to be *always* or *often* a spontaneous response to the circumstances of the moment. Compared to Boomers (28% always + often) and Elders (15%), more Gen-Xers (37%) and Millennials (45%) say spontaneity is a core feature of generosity. Pastors, in contrast, are least likely among the groups surveyed to say so: Just one in five say generosity is *always* (2%) or *often* (18%) spur-of-the-moment.

The notion that generosity is best expressed on the spur of the moment indicates a different set of expectations among

GENEROSITY IS "SPUR-OF-THE-MOMENT"

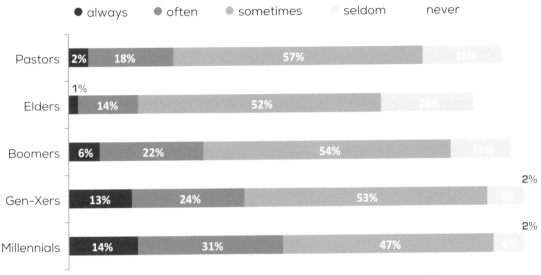

● always   ● often   ● sometimes   ● seldom   ● never

	always	often	sometimes	seldom	never
Pastors	2%	18%	57%	18%	
Elders	1%	14%	52%	20%	
Boomers	6%	22%	54%	15%	
Gen-Xers	13%	24%	53%	6%	2%
Millennials	14%	31%	47%	6%	2%

June 2016, n=606 U.S. Protestant senior pastors;
July 2016, n=1,556 U.S. interested Christians.

younger Christians that will likely lead to fundraising headwinds for churches and organizations that depend on routine, systematic or planned giving and volunteering.

Elders appear to have more cerebral, less circumstantial, ideals related to generosity, especially compared to Millennials. For example, adults over 70 are more likely to say generosity is a discipline (62% vs. 51% Millennials) and is planned (43% vs. 31%). This signals a transition from thinking to feeling in how people process their ideas and impulses related to generosity.

Can generosity turn sour? In other words, what do people think might change a potential act of generosity such that it is no longer truly generous? According to pastors, the attitude of the giver is the biggest factor. Pastors' responses to an open-ended question fall into a handful of general categories, with nearly all focused on the giver's motivations. One in four ministers offers an answer related to guilt or compulsion, and one in six says either selfishness or grudging unwillingness undermine potential generosity.

THE MOST GENEROUS THINGS A PERSON CAN DO

Respondents could choose up to three.

● all Christians   ● Elders   ● Boomers   ● Gen-Xers   ● Millennials

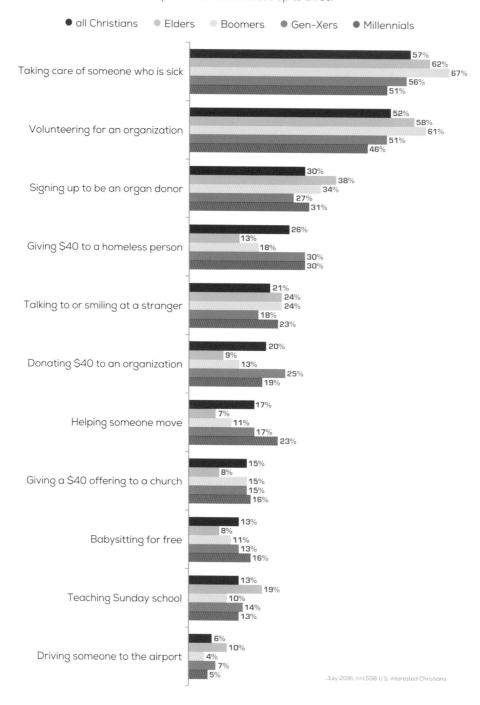

Taking care of someone who is sick
- 57%
- 62%
- 67%
- 56%
- 51%

Volunteering for an organization
- 52%
- 58%
- 61%
- 51%
- 46%

Signing up to be an organ donor
- 30%
- 38%
- 34%
- 27%
- 31%

Giving $40 to a homeless person
- 26%
- 13%
- 18%
- 30%
- 30%

Talking to or smiling at a stranger
- 21%
- 24%
- 24%
- 18%
- 23%

Donating $40 to an organization
- 20%
- 9%
- 13%
- 25%
- 19%

Helping someone move
- 17%
- 7%
- 11%
- 17%
- 23%

Giving a $40 offering to a church
- 15%
- 8%
- 15%
- 15%
- 16%

Babysitting for free
- 13%
- 8%
- 11%
- 13%
- 16%

Teaching Sunday school
- 13%
- 19%
- 10%
- 14%
- 13%

Driving someone to the airport
- 6%
- 10%
- 4%
- 7%
- 5%

July 2016, n=1,556 U.S. interested Christians.

Interestingly, U.S. adults in the qualitative interviews—which included people of various religious backgrounds—were not as convinced as pastors about the importance of intentions. More than half told researchers that buying something for oneself at, for example, Warby Parker or Toms Shoes ("one-to-one" retailers that give away one product to someone in need for every one purchased) is still generous because the *effect*, regardless of the giver's *intent*, is good.

Yet some acts of generosity *are* perceived to be more generous than others. Barna asked participants in the quantitative study to select, from a list of possibilities, the three acts they consider to be most generous. A majority in each generation believes taking care of a sick person is one of the most generous things one can do. Boomers are most likely to express this perception—which is notable because they are also most likely to be caring for aging parents.

Similarly, volunteering *for an organization* is considered highly generous by a large share of each age cohort—yet a significantly smaller percentage views volunteering *for a person* (for example, driving them to the airport or babysitting for free) to be exceptionally generous. Analysis suggests this disparity may have something to do with people's perceptions of personal cost—that actions requiring more effort tend to be perceived as more generous. For example, volunteering for an organization often requires specialized training, adherence to a set of rules and expectations and a specific time commitment, compared to helping a friend or family member. A similar finding supports this insight: Many people consider giving $40 to a homeless person more generous than giving $40 to an organization or church. The dollar amount is the same in each case, but the cost of a personal encounter with a homeless teen or adult tends to be higher than tucking a check in the offering basket when it passes by.

CHRISTIAN GENEROSITY

When it comes to the most important reason for Christians to be generous, there are some gaps between pastors and parishioners.

Pastors say the giver's wrong attitude can change an action from potentially generous to no longer generous

THE MOST IMPORTANT REASON FOR CHRISTIANS TO BE GENEROUS

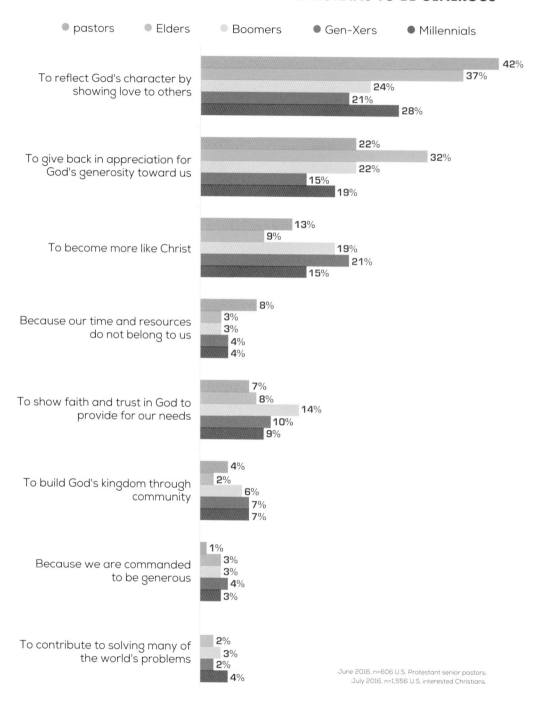

● pastors ● Elders ● Boomers ● Gen-Xers ● Millennials

To reflect God's character by showing love to others
- 42%
- 37%
- 24%
- 21%
- 28%

To give back in appreciation for God's generosity toward us
- 22%
- 32%
- 22%
- 15%
- 19%

To become more like Christ
- 13%
- 9%
- 19%
- 21%
- 15%

Because our time and resources do not belong to us
- 8%
- 3%
- 3%
- 4%
- 4%

To show faith and trust in God to provide for our needs
- 7%
- 8%
- 14%
- 10%
- 9%

To build God's kingdom through community
- 4%
- 2%
- 6%
- 7%
- 7%

Because we are commanded to be generous
- 1%
- 3%
- 3%
- 4%
- 3%

To contribute to solving many of the world's problems
- 2%
- 3%
- 2%
- 4%

June 2016, n=606 U.S. Protestant senior pastors,
July 2016, n=1,556 U.S. interested Christians.

For example, a plurality of pastors—more than two in five—say the most important reason is "to reflect God's character by showing love to others." More than one-third of Elders agrees with pastors, but the total of all Christians who select that answer is just 25 percent. Gen-Xers, for their part, are half as likely as pastors to say reflecting God's character is the main reason.

On the other hand, more Gen-Xers and Boomers than pastors and Elders believe "to become more like Christ" is the most important reason for Christian generosity. And Elders are an outlier in their choice of giving back "in appreciation for God's generosity toward us," with one-third resonating with this option compared to one in six younger Christians and one in five pastors.

In short, while each of the options is biblically defensible and broadly orthodox, the spread of findings shows little consensus among Christians and their pastors on why, exactly, they should be generous.

But how do Christians actually become generous? Academic research has indicated that parental modeling is a major factor,[4] and responses to this study appear to bolster those findings.

Perceptions of their parents' generosity correlate with how important generosity is to Christians in adulthood

CORRELATIONS BETWEEN PERCEPTIONS OF PARENTS' GENEROSITY & IMPORTANCE OF GENEROSITY

How generous were your parents?	How important is generosity to you?			
	% extremely	% very	% somewhat	% not very / not at all
Extremely	40	11	9	3
Very	32	46	27	22
Somewhat	17	34	51	46
Not very / not at all	11	9	12	29

July 2016, n=1,556 U.S. interested Christians.

Christians' perceptions of their parents' generosity during their childhood correlate with generosity's importance to them as adults.

DISCIPLING FOR GENEROSITY

The gap is immense between pastors and the average Christian on the question of whether it is acceptable for a church member to substitute volunteering for financial giving. Pastors, on the whole, disagree that these two forms of generosity are interchangeable. More than eight out of 10 disagree strongly (67%) or somewhat (18%) that "it is okay for a member who volunteers extensively not to give financially." But just one in five Christians is on the same page with pastors (10% strongly, 11% somewhat disagree).

IT IS OKAY FOR MEMBERS TO VOLUNTEER FOR THEIR CHURCH INSTEAD OF GIVING FINANCIALLY

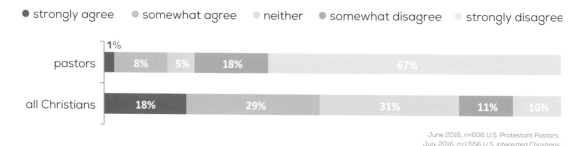

● strongly agree ● somewhat agree ● neither ● somewhat disagree ● strongly disagree

pastors 1%	8%	5%	18%	67%
all Christians	18%	29%	31%	11%	10%

June 2016, n=606 U.S. Protestant Pastors; July 2016, n=1,556 U.S. interested Christians.

> By their own estimates, pastors talk about volunteering much more often than they talk about financial giving

Ironically, some parishioners' confusion on this question may come from pastors themselves. Only 39 percent of pastors say they or other leaders speak from the pulpit about tithing or giving to the church at least once a month (17% once per month, 22% multiple times per month). But more than six in 10 say they or other leaders speak from the pulpit at least once a month on the topic of volunteering (35% once, 27% multiple times). So, by their own estimates, pastors talk about volunteering much more often than they talk about financial giving. Thus, it's no surprise that at least some of their congregants believe serving is an acceptable substitute for tithing.

Before church leaders cut back on the amount of time they spend talking about volunteerism and serving, however, it's important to note that serving and financial giving appear to go hand in hand. (So consider talking *more* about giving rather than *less* about serving!) As the chart shows, Christians who give most are also most likely to say they have volunteered within the past week or month. The pattern also holds true for those who consider generosity extremely important.

Those who give more are most likely to spend time serving others—but they are also more likely to say generosity is a frequent topic of conversation in their family. (Modeling again!) Two-thirds of Christians who consider generosity to be extremely important say they talked with their spouse (67%) or children (64%) about generosity within the past week, compared to fewer than half of all others. It appears that generosity is developed at home—good news for churches structured to support families.

Serving and financial giving appear to go hand in hand

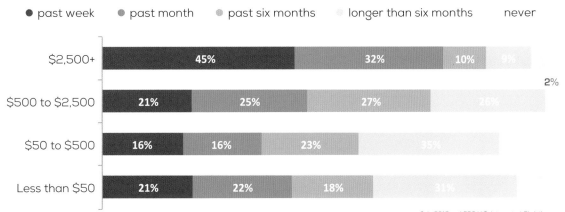

THE LAST TIME I VOLUNTEERED, BY REPORTED ANNUAL GIVING

● past week   ● past month   ● past six months   longer than six months   never

	past week	past month	past six months	longer than six months	never
$2,500+	45%	32%	10%	9%	2%
$500 to $2,500	21%	25%	27%	26%	
$50 to $500	16%	16%	23%	35%	
Less than $50	21%	22%	18%	31%	

July 2016, *n*=1,556 U.S. interested Christians.

Generations & Generosity

Different generations gravitate to different kinds of generous acts. For example, half of all Elders, the oldest adults, say volunteering or serving others is the most generous type of action. But Boomers, their middle-aged counterparts, are split on whether serving or offering emotional support is supremely generous, and Millennials are much more likely than all older adults to say showing hospitality epitomizes generosity. The challenge for church leaders is obvious: How do you create an intergenerational community of people who can't even agree on how to be generous to each other? Here's a breakdown by generation of the kinds of actions Christians think are most generous.

 Elders   Boomers   Gen-Xers   Millennials

Serving / Volunteering

A majority of Elders think serving others is the most generous action a person can take. Smaller, but still significant, percentages of Boomers, Gen-Xers and Millennials agree.

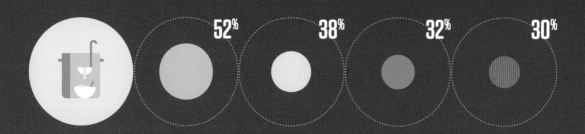

52%   38%   32%   30%

Offering Emotional / Relational Support

Roughly three in 10 Boomers, Gen-Xers and Millennials say emotional care is most generous—but only one in six Elders agree.

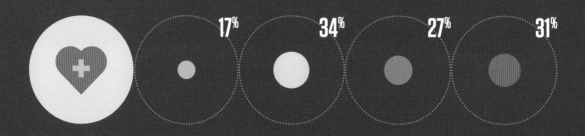

17%   34%   27%   31%

Donating Money

Financial giving ranks third on Christians' list of most generous actions, but lower for Millennials.

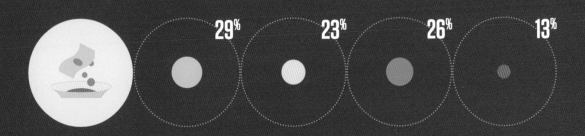

29% 23% 26% 13%

Showing Hospitality

One in five Millennials believes being hospitable is the most generous act.

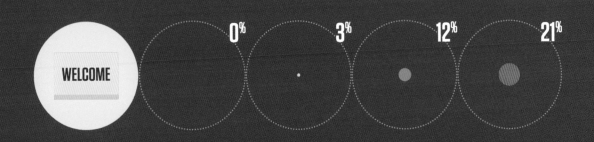

WELCOME

0% 3% 12% 21%

Giving Gifts

A handful of Christians from each generation say a gift is the highest expression of generosity.

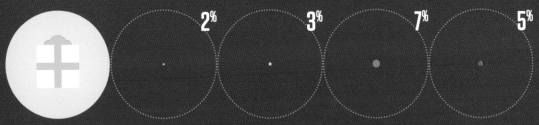

2% 3% 7% 5%

July 2016, *n*=1,556 U.S. interested Christians.

2. THE HEART GAP

KEY FINDINGS

- Millennials are more likely than older adults to think of generosity in terms of hospitality and less in terms of money.
- Service or volunteerism is highly valued and more frequently practiced by Elders.
- People tend to think their preferred way of expressing generosity is more generous than other ways.
- Just one in 10 Christians say "to serve God with my money" is their ultimate financial goal.

Researchers asked what actions people believe qualify as "giving to others." While there is generally broad agreement about the *spirit* of generosity, people differ when it comes to envisioning an *act* of generosity. "Service" (32%) and "emotional / relational support" (30%) are the two most popular options, with about one in three U.S. Christians saying they strongly associate actions that fall into these categories with the concept of "giving to others." About one in five says giving money is the action they most associate with the phrase (22%), while fewer say "hospitality" (12%) or "gifts" (5%). To be clear, donating money is in third place, and only one-fifth of adults select it as their top expression of "giving to others."

The findings reveal gaps by gender and by generation on this question. Women and men are about equally likely to associate gifts and service with giving to others, but women more strongly associate acts of emotional or relational support with generosity

(36% vs. 22% men) while men have a greater tendency than women to choose giving money (27% vs. 17% women).

Even more significant than gender differences, each generation seems to have their own set of associations. Millennials, for example, are on par with the norm when it comes to service, emotional or relational support, and gifts. But the percentages for money (13% vs. 22% all Christians) and hospitality (21% vs. 12%) are essentially flipped: Millennials prioritize hospitality far more than money as an expression of generosity. At a different extreme are Elders, who are much more likely than the average to strongly associate service with generosity (52% vs. 32% all) and not at all likely to choose hospitality (less than 1 percent of Elder respondents chose this option).

Researchers asked people to define these categories in their own words, and some interesting themes emerged from their responses. Most think the concepts of "welcome" and "openness" broadly encompass the idea of hospitality, while only about one-third limits the definition to hosting in one's home. This more

> Women more strongly associate acts of emotional or relational support with generosity

TYPES OF ACTIONS STRONGLY ASSOCIATED WITH GENEROSITY

● all Christians ● Elders ● Boomers ● Gen-Xers ● Millennials

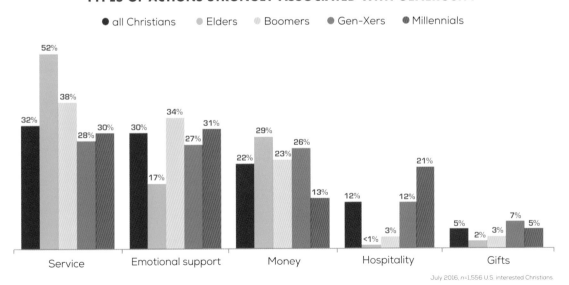

July 2016, n=1,556 U.S. interested Christians.

general, rather than specific, notion may account for hospitality's popularity among Millennials, who tend more than other generations to value openness and unqualified acceptance.

In what ways are Christians most often generous to others? Researchers found that people most strongly associate their own chosen means of expressing generosity with their ideal of generosity. That is, people walk their talk. If they believe monetary giving is the best way to be generous, they give money. If they believe serving is the best way, they tend to give through acts of service. Three out of five people who practice generosity by offering emotional or relational support to others generally associate acts of relational support with generosity.

Serving or volunteering and offering relational support are the most common expressions of generosity across generations, but percentages vary, likely related in some instances to free time and financial situation. Elders, for example—many of whom are retired or no longer working full time—are the age cohort by far most likely to report expressing generosity in service or volunteerism. And Millennials, who tend to have fewer overall financial

Only one-third of people limits the definition of "hospitality" to hosting in one's home; others think the concepts of "welcome" and "openness" get closer to the idea

PEOPLE CONSIDER THEIR PREFERRED ACTS OF GENEROSITY TO BE MOST GENEROUS

In what way are you most often generous to others?	Which type of giving do you personally see as most strongly associated with generosity?				
	% Money	% Emotional / relational support	% Gifts	% Hospitality	% Service
Monetary support	40	6	9	8	12
Emotional / relational support	17	62	19	15	23
Gifts	12	7	54	10	8
Hospitality	10	9	7	46	5
Service / volunteering	17	12	8	20	49

July 2016, n=1,556 U.S. interested Christians.

MOST FREQUENT PERSONAL EXPRESSION OF GENEROSITY

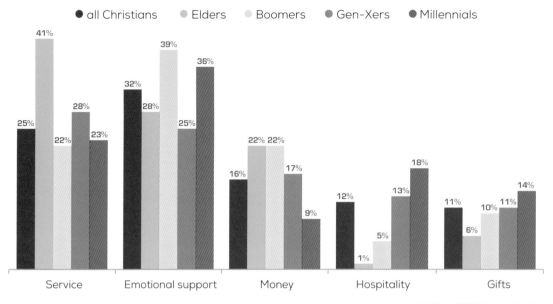

● all Christians   ● Elders   ● Boomers   ● Gen-Xers   ● Millennials

July 2016, n=1,556 U.S. interested Christians.

resources, are least likely to say they most often express generosity through monetary giving.

According to the 2015 National Time Use Survey, Gen-Xers are the generation most likely to volunteer (28%) and Millennials are least likely (19%). However, when *hours* of service are accounted for, Boomers and Elders 65 and older pull ahead of young adults: Older Americans volunteer an average of 94 hours annually, more than twice the average of 36 hours among people under 35.[5]

In the Barna survey, pastors were asked to select as many expressions of generosity as they believed applied to them. Like other Christians (Elders excepted), relational support is pastors' most frequent act of generosity (86%), followed by giving money (77%), giving gifts (61%) and extending hospitality (58%).

SERVING & SUPPORTING PEOPLE

According to the Bureau of Labor Statistics, roughly 7 percent of adults volunteer on any given day in America. Those who serve

> The way a person is most often generous to others is also the type of giving he or she most associates with generosity

usually spend between two and three hours at a stretch doing their volunteer activity.[6] In this study, Barna found that engaging in the act of volunteering correlates with a perception that doing so is generous; that is, if a person has volunteered their time on behalf of an organization within the past six months, he or she is more likely to associate volunteering with generosity. And the reverse is also true: People who have *not* volunteered are less likely than those who have to think of volunteering as particularly generous.

When people think about their acts of generosity, they think beyond volunteering for organizations. Some participants in the qualitative interviews mentioned taking care of people inside or outside of their household—or both—and labor statistics confirm that between 10 and 25 percent of Americans engage in caregiving on an average weekday.[7] Other interview participants mentioned "picking up slack at work," singing at funerals, doing housework for extended family members and assisting with meal preparation.

People who do not volunteer are less likely than those who do to think of volunteering as generous

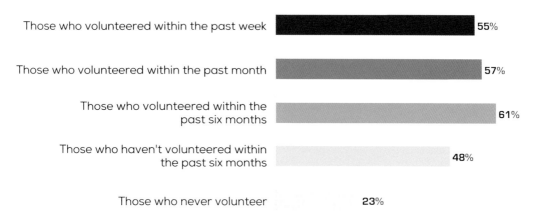

BELIEVE VOLUNTEERING IS AN ACT OF GENEROSITY

Those who volunteered within the past week — 55%

Those who volunteered within the past month — 57%

Those who volunteered within the past six months — 61%

Those who haven't volunteered within the past six months — 48%

Those who never volunteer — 23%

July 2016, *n*=1,556 U.S. interested Christians; respondents chose "volunteering for an organization" from a list of options.

The spectrum of actions people consider to be generous is wide—especially when they are thinking about their own actions

Somewhat similar are acts people identify under the category "emotional / relational generosity." The main difference seems to lie in the planned nature of volunteering contrasted with a spontaneous approach to relational support, which people seem more often to offer in the midst of daily interactions. For example, one interviewee said, "I listen when others are hurting." Another reported, "I use social media to support friends and charities." And still another said offering advice is a way she is emotionally generous. One respondent said "allowing you to merge into traffic" was his act of relational generosity, and still another said he likes "saying hello to people I don't know, but acting as if I do"—an act that, for the recipient, may baffle more than delight.

Some acts described by interview participants under the label "hospitality" are in the same thematic ballpark. Rather than limiting the concept of hospitality to hosting, many respondents described actions taken outside the home. One said, "I buy lunch most often. I inquire about others' lives and try to remember important things they tell me." Another, a cashier, reported a different way she is hospitable: "Smile and be kind to strangers that I meet in daily errands and while working, especially if they are not nice first." And yet another described "holding the door for someone, getting something for someone who can't reach, allowing someone to go ahead of you in the grocery store."

In short, the spectrum of actions people consider to be generous is wide—especially when they are thinking about their *own* actions.

GIVING GIFTS & MONEY

One respondent had a unique take on gift giving: "Sharing my food, cigarettes and drinks with my coworkers." While there may be potential drawbacks to some gifts (cigarettes, for example), neither pastors nor Christians seem to believe that a gift's desirability—or not—is what makes it generous. Rather, it is still the thought that counts.

Cigarettes aside, gift giving is a part of American culture with its own schedule and social obligations. For example, Christmas and birthdays are common occasions to give gifts and, often, to expect to receive them. Despite these social expectations, some interviewees said that giving gifts on these occasions is an act of generosity.

Many Americans donate money on a similar "schedule," especially during the end-of-year holiday season. Accouting for these occasions and all other donating throughout the years, how much do they give?

When it comes to donations, self-reported giving is not usually as reliable as reviewing actual tax-return data—but the latter was not an option open to the research team! So Barna asked respondents to report how much money they donated to their church or other nonprofits last year, expecting that the resulting

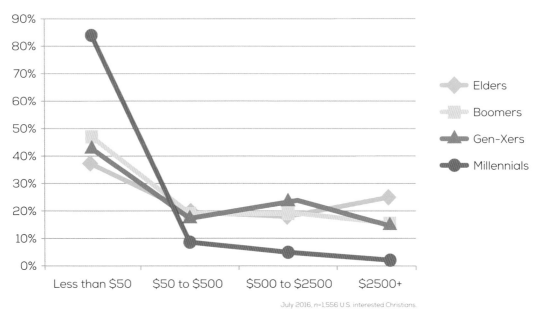

SELF-REPORTED DONATIONS FOR LAST YEAR, BY GENERATION

July 2016, n=1,556 U.S. interested Christians.

data might be more useful to gauge Christians' self-perceptions than to measure actual monetary giving.

However, researchers found that respondents' self-reported donations approximate the amounts predicted by age, churchgoing habits and marital status. Younger adults tend to earn less money, to attend church less often (or not at all) and to be unmarried—and 84 percent of Millennials report donating less than $50 during the past year, more than twice the percentage of Elders who say so (37%). Middle-aged and older adults tend to earn more, to attend church more often and to be married, and their self-reported giving is only a bit higher than what researchers would expect, given these factors.

The U.S. Bureau of Economic Analysis reports the average American has $39,424 in annual disposable income (that is, the amount that remains after taxes are paid).[8] According to analysis of data Barna gathered between 2013 and 2016, practicing Christians report giving an average (median) of $1,400 a year to their church—thus, between 3 and 4 percent of their disposable income. More than half of all Christians in *The Generosity Gap* study say they gave less than $500 last year, and 15 percent did not donate at all. So the $1,400 "per person" is not evenly spread across the Christian population; some are giving much more, and some much less.

Aside from any specific theology about tithing, most leaders will agree than $1,400 a year is modest compared to the economic capacity of the average person of faith. An examination of Christians' priorities for money reveals one reason why: Of 10 possible answers to the question, "What would you consider to be the ultimate financial goal in life?" the option "to serve God with my money" ranks at number six, with just one in 10 Christians choosing that answer. Serving God with one's money is, for most people, not as urgent as other priorities—though Elders are twice as likely as others to say it is, which makes serving God the number-one financial goal among senior Christians. The percentage of Elders whose goal is "to have enough money to give charitably" is also higher than average (18% vs. 11% all Christians).

Just 1 in 10 Christians says that "serving God with my money" is their ultimate financial goal

"Providing for my family" tops the list among all Christians (22%), and Millennials are more likely than the norm to select this option (31%). Since many young adults are starting their family (or at least contemplating it), it makes sense that this obligation would be on their minds. It's less clear whether this is a true generational difference or if Millennials' goals will change over time.

These differences show that a Christian audience—especially one that is intergenerational—will hear teaching and other messaging about money through a variety of personal filters. For all but the small percentage of Christians that already views money primarily

A Christian audience will hear teaching about money through a variety of filters

THE ULTIMATE FINANCIAL GOAL FOR LIFE, BY GENERATION

	% all Christians	% Millennials	% Gen-Xers	% Boomers	% Elders
1. Provide for my family	22	31	18	18	13
2. Support the lifestyle I want	15	14	17	13	7
3. Meet my obligations and needs	13	8	15	15	16
4. Be content	13	11	14	13	14
5. Give charitably	11	8	11	15	18
6. Serve God with my money	**10**	**10**	**9**	**11**	**19**
7. Establish a financial legacy	7	7	8	6	6
8. Be debt-free	6	6	5	6	4
9. Show my talent / hard work	2	4	1	1	-
10. Other	2	1	2	2	4

July 2016, n=1,556 U.S. interested Christians.

as an opportunity to serve God, teaching on biblical generosity will have to start with *why* to give, not *how* to give.

For many, money is about caring for loved ones or giving to the Church. For others, it is about lifestyle and personal contentment. We'll return to these distinctions in the next chapter as a helpful lens for understanding a variety of giving behaviors and attitudes—and why this is a challenging gap to close.

HOW GENERATIONS PERCEIVE THEMSELVES

Many Millennials prioritize practical concerns over philanthropic goals when it comes to their financial plans, yet generosity remains a significant facet of their self-concept. Of the four adult generations of Christians, Millennials are most likely to say that generosity is important to them personally. Boomers are less apt to say so, and twice as likely as the youngest adults to say generosity is only *somewhat* or *not very* important to them (39% vs. 20% Millennials).

Generosity appears to be important to most Christians, but how well aligned are their giving practices with their priorities? Researchers have found that asking survey-takers to view themselves through the eyes of another person often yields a

> Teaching on biblical generosity will have to start with *why* to give, not *how* to give

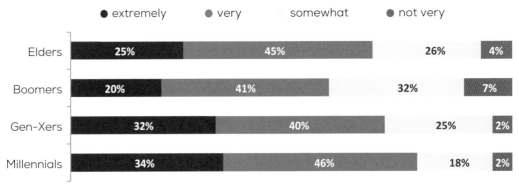

THE IMPORTANCE OF GENEROSITY TO ME, BY GENERATION

● extremely   ● very   somewhat   ● not very

Generation	extremely	very	somewhat	not very
Elders	25%	45%	26%	4%
Boomers	20%	41%	32%	7%
Gen-Xers	32%	40%	25%	2%
Millennials	34%	46%	18%	2%

July 2016, *n*=1,556 U.S. interested Christians.

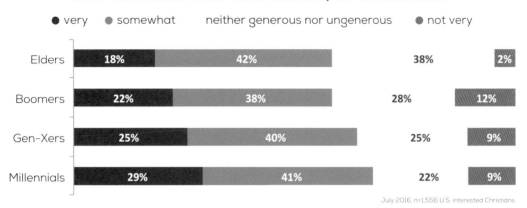

HOW GENEROUS I AM WITH MONEY, BY GENERATION

● very ● somewhat ● neither generous nor ungenerous ● not very

	very	somewhat	neither generous nor ungenerous	not very
Elders	18%	42%	38%	2%
Boomers	22%	38%	28%	12%
Gen-Xers	25%	40%	25%	9%
Millennials	29%	41%	22%	9%

July 2016. n=1,556 U.S. interested Christians.

more honest response. So Barna asked, "If your friends knew everything about your finances and giving habits, how would they rate your generosity?"

Millennials are slightly more prone than their older counterparts to say their friends would rate them as *very* generous, while Elders are least likely to say this. Twelve percent of Boomers, meanwhile, say their friends would rate them as *not very* generous, six times the percentage of Elders who say so. A plurality in each generation says they are *somewhat* generous.

As explored in the previous section, Millennials are most likely of the generations to report donating less than $50 last year. Yet here we see that three in 10 would rate themselves as *very* generous with their monetary giving. What's going on here? Analysis suggests Millennials think they are generous *relative to their income level and life stage*—but they also recognize, as we'll see below, that older generations often have greater resources and therefore tend to give more.

HOW GENERATIONS PERCEIVE EACH OTHER

Understanding the different ways generations think about life, values and priorities can be helpful for any leader trying to create and sustain intergenerational community. At the same time, if we hold

> The "heart gap" created by stubborn generational stereotypes presents a pastoral challenge

too tightly to our generational stereotypes, the "generation gap" becomes merely a cultural trope that has outlived its usefulness, a convenient excuse for divisions rather than a starting point for greater understanding. In a few findings from this study, the latter appears to be the case—and the "heart gap" created by stubborn generational stereotypes presents a pastoral challenge to leaders.

Barna asked Christians about the generations in their church congregation: Which is most generous with money, time and hospitality? The answers reveal a high degree of generational loyalty among older Christians but less consistent perceptions among younger adults.

The older three generations (Gen-Xers, Boomers and Elders) believe that, out of all the age groups in their church, Boomers give money most sacrificially—but among Gen-Xers only about one-third says so, compared to majorities of both Boomers and Elders. The greater part of Millennials is nearly split on whether Boomers or Gen-Xers are most sacrificial in their giving, but one in five says

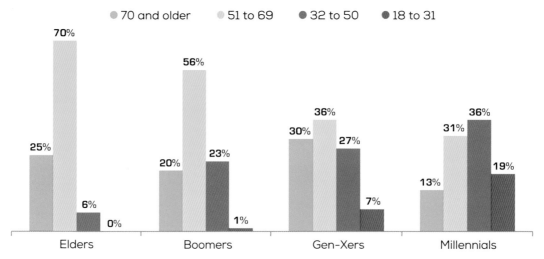

WHICH GENERATION IN YOUR CHURCH GIVES MONEY MOST SACRIFICIALLY?

● 70 and older   ● 51 to 69   ● 32 to 50   ● 18 to 31

Elders: 25%, 70%, 6%, 0%
Boomers: 20%, 56%, 23%, 1%
Gen-Xers: 30%, 36%, 27%, 7%
Millennials: 13%, 31%, 36%, 19%

July 2016, n=1,556 U.S. interested Christians.

their own generation sacrifices most when it comes to financial giving. Fewer than one in 20 among the older generations agrees.

As with financial giving, most Christians perceive Boomers to be most sacrificial with their time, and the percentage that believes Millennials to be most generous in this regard shrinks in each successively older generation. Thirty-five percent of Millennials say their age cohort is most sacrificial when it comes to time, compared to one in seven Gen-Xers, one in 10 Boomers and just 3 percent of Elders. There are, of course, many ways to be generous with time beyond formal volunteering. But according to the American Time Use Survey, a lower percentage of Millennials and a higher percentage of Elders volunteers on any given day, compared to other generations.[9]

When it comes to hospitality, more than three-quarters of Christians over 50 say older adults are strongest in this area; two-thirds of Gen-Xers agree that Boomers and Elders in their church are most hospitable. Millennials, meanwhile, consistent with

A lower percentage of Millennials and a higher percentage of Elders volunteers on any given day, compared to other generations

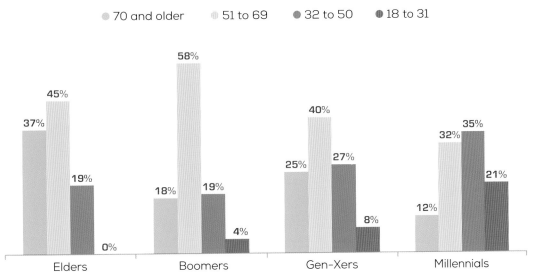

WHICH GENERATION IN YOUR CHURCH IS MOST HOSPITABLE?

- 70 and older
- 51 to 69
- 32 to 50
- 18 to 31

Elders: 37%, 45%, 19%, 0%

Boomers: 18%, 58%, 19%, 4%

Gen-Xers: 25%, 40%, 27%, 8%

Millennials: 12%, 32%, 35%, 21%

July 2016, n=1,556 U.S. interested Christians.

their definition of generosity, give themselves high marks here. Because openness and welcome are of such high value to younger adults, and more broadly in an increasingly contentious society, hospitality is a potential avenue for reverse mentoring, wherein older Christians learn from younger believers. Taking a learning, rather than teaching, posture could be an older Christian's most generous act.

NARROWING THE HEART GAP

Imagine that a twentysomething Christian, Rachel, hears a Sunday message about generosity, and decides to be more intentional about acts she perceives to be generous. So she begins to host weekly home-cooked dinners for a few single coworkers who live far from home, and invites a friend to sleep on her couch until the friend can find an affordable place of her own. She joins a cultural exchange club to get to know people who have different beliefs and backgrounds, and practices listening to their stories so they feel heard and understood.

Folks from the older generations in Rachel's church—a group that likely includes her pastor, since the average Protestant pastor is over 50[10]—may not see these actions as a legitimate response to the call for greater generosity. Neither her financial contributions to the church nor the number of hours she serves have increased. According to their perceptions of generosity and preferences for different kinds of generous actions, Rachel is failing to mature as a generous Christian.

If not navigated wisely, the "heart gap" detailed in this section has the potential to alienate Christians of different ages from each other. But it doesn't have to be that way—we don't have to be slaves to our stereotypes. As David Kinnaman explores in the conclusion to *The Generosity Gap*, these differences offer Christians an opportunity to practice generosity in ways that create deeper and more resilient intergenerational unity.

Generational differences on generosity have the potential to alienate Christians from each other. But it doesn't have to be that way

Open-Handed vs. Tight-Fisted

Givers

Givers' ultimate financial goal is focused on God or other people.

Provide for my family **43%**

20% Serve God with my money

Give charit-ably **23%**

14% Leave a legacy for others

Two-thirds of Givers are married.

65% Married

21% Never married

14% Other singles

57% of Christians who attended church during the past week are Givers.

42% strongly agree that every member should financially support their church.

30% say Christians should give 10% or more of their income.

One-third gave at least $500 last year; 14% gave $2,500 or more.

1 in 4 Givers sets aside 10% or more of their income for their church or a nonprofit.

Do motives make a difference? They sure do. Christians whose ultimate financial goal is centered on serving God or providing for others tend to be open-handed with their resources (Givers), while those whose goal is self-focused are more likely to hold on to their money (Keepers).

Keepers

Keepers' ultimate financial goal is centered on themselves.

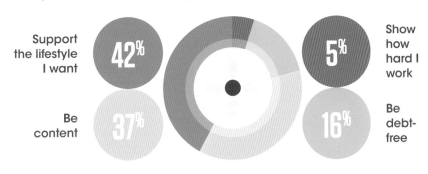

Support the lifestyle I want **42%**

Be content **37%**

Show how hard I work **5%**

Be debt-free **16%**

Half of Keepers are single.

49% Married

31% Never married

20% Other singles

30% of Christians who attended church in the past week are Keepers.

30% strongly agree that every member should financially support their church.

22% say Christians should give 10% or more of their income.

Less than one-quarter gave at least $500 last year; 8% gave $2,500 or more.

1 in 7 Keepers sets aside 10% or more of their income for their church or a nonprofit.

July 2016, n=1,556 U.S. interested Christians.

3. THE SOUL GAP

KEY FINDINGS

- A person's ultimate financial goal strongly correlates with his or her giving habits.
- Givers are more likely to be married, to have children and to be Protestant, while Keepers are more likely to be single, not to have children and to live in a city.
- Orthodox Christian beliefs and regular church attendance correlate with more generous giving habits.

The previous chapter looked briefly at what Christians say about their ultimate financial goal for life. To find out if these "soul motivations" are connected to behaviors and attitudes related to financial giving—and, if so, what it may mean for cultivating Christian generosity—Barna analysts created two groups:

- **Givers** are motivated by "others-focused" goals: to provide for their family (43% of Givers), to give charitably (23%) to serve God with their money (20%) or to leave a legacy for others (14%). Fifty percent of Christians are Givers.

- **Keepers** are motivated by "self-focused" goals: to support the lifestyle they want (42% of Keepers), to be content (37%), to be debt-free (16%) or to earn enough to show how hard they work (5%). Thirty-five percent of Christians are Keepers.

Fifteen percent of respondents don't fall into either category because they are primarily motivated to meet their financial

obligations, which researchers categorize as an "indeterminate" goal.* In an analysis of employment status, household income and how these uncategorized respondents perceive their financial situation, researchers discovered they are more likely than Givers or Keepers to be unemployed and earn less than $50,000 per year, and to say they are "struggling to keep up with day-to-day expenses." So for many, if not most, their ultimate goal is a reflection of real and present financial struggles, not of a spiritual mindset or a gap in effective discipleship. This needs-focused group is excluded from analysis in this chapter, since their primary financial goal does not appear to drive their giving behaviors or views on generosity. (In fact, though they tend to earn less than Keepers, they often give more.)

For the other 85 percent of Christians who are either Givers or Keepers, ultimate financial goals correlate to both generous habits and perspectives on generosity—perhaps the most important gap revealed by this research. Here's the big takeaway right up front: *Christians with giving goals give a lot, and Christians with keeping goals give less or not at all.* The challenge for leaders is not to coax Keepers to give more, but to help them close the soul gap and become Givers from the inside out.

Let's get to know these two groups.

WHO THEY ARE (DEMOGRAPHICS)

As we saw in chapter 2, Millennials are more likely than other generations, by a significant margin, to prioritize providing for a family above other financial goals (31% vs. 18% Gen-Xers and Boomers, 13% Elders). Elders, by contrast, are most likely to say serving God with their money is their ultimate goal (19% vs. ~10% all others). These outlier percentages push more Millennials and Elders into the Giver category than their middle-aged counterparts.

When it comes to household income, Givers are not giving more because they make more. In fact, Keepers tend to be somewhat more financially comfortable than Givers: 45 percent earn

> The challenge for leaders is not to coax Keepers to give more, but to become Givers from the inside out

---

*Also included are the 2 percent of respondents who chose "other" from the list of options.

GIVERS AND KEEPERS, BY GENERATION

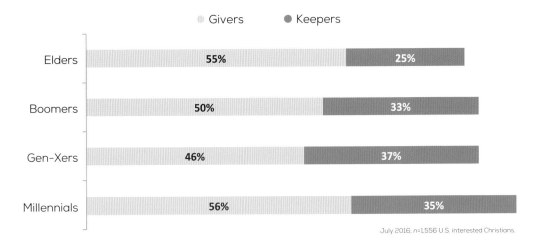

Givers   Keepers

	Givers	Keepers
Elders	55%	25%
Boomers	50%	33%
Gen-Xers	46%	37%
Millennials	56%	35%

July 2016, n=1,556 U.S. interested Christians.

more than $75,000 per year compared to 39 percent of Givers. Some of this disparity may be due to the fact that Keepers (37%) are more likely than Givers (30%) to live in a city, where incomes are sometimes higher to cover steeper living expenses. Relatedly, Christians in the Northeast are more likely than those in other regions to prioritize keeping goals; Keepers (44%) actually outnumber Givers (42%) among Christians in that region.

Asian Christians are more likely than other ethnicities to be Givers (60% vs. ~50% all others). In an analysis of Asian respondents' answers to the question of financial goals, Barna found they are slightly more likely than white, Hispanic and black Christians to prioritize any of the giving goals; that is, higher percentages of Asians say they want to provide for family, donate to charity, leave a legacy or serve God with their money, compared to Christians of other ethnic backgrounds.

There is no significant difference between Givers and Keepers on educational attainment, but marital status is a different story: Givers are more likely to be married (65%), while Keepers are more often single (51%). It's also slightly more common for Givers to have children under 18 living at home (47% vs. 41%). It appears

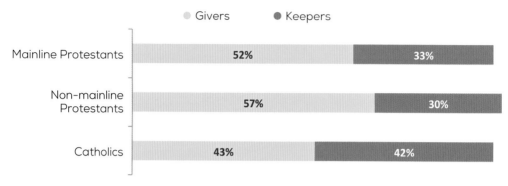

GIVERS AND KEEPERS, BY CHRISTIAN TRADITION

● Givers   ● Keepers

	Givers	Keepers
Mainline Protestants	52%	33%
Non-mainline Protestants	57%	30%
Catholics	43%	42%

July 2016, n=1,556 U.S. interested Christians.

that, at least in the U.S. where increasing numbers of people choose not to marry or have children, the family remains a crucible where self-focus can be transmuted to putting others' needs first.

Last in the realm of demographics, a Christian's faith tradition appears to influence whether they are a Giver or a Keeper. Protestants overall, and especially non-mainline Protestants—a category that includes denominations often identified as "evangelical"—are more likely to be Givers, while Catholics are about evenly split between Givers and Keepers.

WHAT THEY PRACTICE & BELIEVE (THEOLOGRAPHICS)

Barna has found that religious beliefs and faith practices ("theolographics") are often just as predictive of people's behavior and perceptions as demographics—if not more so. This trend holds true when it comes to Givers and Keepers.

Regarding faith practices, regular church attendance strongly correlates with giving goals. Nearly six in 10 Christians who attended a worship service within the past week are Givers (57%), compared to 45 percent of Christians who did not. There is virtually no daylight between those who attended within the past

Regular church
attendance strongly
correlates with
giving goals

month (44% are Givers) and those for whom it has been longer than six months (45%); only weekly church involvement appears to make a significant difference.

With regard to religious beliefs, Christians who align with traditional orthodoxy are more likely to be Givers. (Or it may be that Givers are more likely to profess orthodox beliefs; it's unclear whether financial goals or religious beliefs are causal.) Givers are also more likely to say their faith is very important in their life and to say they sense God actively involved in their day-to-day life.

RELIGIOUS BELIEFS & FAITH PERSPECTIVES, GIVERS VS. KEEPERS

Belief / Perspective	% Givers	% Keepers
"God is the all-powerful, all-knowing, perfect creator of the universe who rules the world today"	83	73
"Your religious faith is very important in your life today" (strongly agree)	66	48
"You sense that God is actively involved with you throughout the day" (always)	50	44
"The Bible is totally accurate in all of the principles it teaches" (strongly agree)	47	27
"When he lived on earth, Jesus Christ was human and committed sins, like other people" (strongly disagree)	40	21
"You, personally, have a responsibility to tell other people your religious beliefs" (strongly agree)	31	17
"The devil, or Satan, is not a living being but is a symbol of evil" (strongly disagree)	31	14
"If a person is generally good, or does enough good things for others during their life, they will earn a place in Heaven" (strongly disagree)	31	11

July 2016, n=1,556 U.S. interested Christians.

One in three Givers says they donated $500 or more last year to their church or other nonprofits (33%), compared to about one in five Keepers (22%); they are nearly twice as likely to report donating $2,500 or more (14% vs. 8%). Plus, they are more likely to report setting their own giving at 10 percent or more of their income (25% vs. 13%).

These findings dovetail with ongoing research Barna has conducted since 2011 with American Bible Society on U.S. adults' level of engagement with the Bible: Those with a higher level of engagement tend to give more. Specifically, the *Bible engaged* have a "high" view of the Scriptures and read the Bible four or more times per week; as of 2017, this group makes up about 20 percent of the U.S. adult population. Compared to those who read the Bible less often or hold "lower" views of the Scriptures, Bible-engaged Americans are far more likely to report donating $2,000 or more to their church or a charity last year (49% vs. 17% Bible friendly, 18% Bible neutral, 13% Bible skeptics).[11]

Those with a higher level of Bible engagement tend to give more

WHAT THEY SAY ABOUT GENEROSITY

Not surprisingly, Givers are more apt to say generosity is *extremely* important to them (33% vs. 24% Keepers) and to believe generosity is *always* a discipline (26% vs. 18%) and a response to Christ's love (53% vs. 43%).

Givers are also more convinced than Keepers of how important it is for Christians to support their home church: 42 percent strongly agree that "every member should give some amount," versus 30 percent of Keepers. Additionally, they are more likely to specify that Christians should give their church 10 percent or more of their income (30% vs. 22%).

When it comes to what category of actions they most strongly associate with generosity, one in five among both Givers (20%) and Keepers (21%) says giving money is most generous. However, Keepers tend most to favor emotional or relational support (37%

vs. 24% Givers) while Givers prefer serving (36% vs. 27%) and, to a lesser extent, hospitality (15% vs. 8%).

Drilling down to specific actions, scenarios that involve a mediating organization seem to have greater appeal for Keepers than for Givers, such as volunteering for a nonprofit (58% Keepers vs. 53% Givers) or donating money to an organization or cause (24% vs. 16%). By contrast, Givers seem to favor actions that demand some level of personal, relational investment, such as taking care of a sick person or teaching Sunday school.

More than one-third of Keepers, however, says emotional or relational support is their go-to mode of generosity (38%) compared to three in 10 Givers (29%)—but they are less inclined than Givers to view more demanding relational acts, such as teaching Sunday school, as supremely generous. Further research is needed to discover what's behind this apparent dissonance.

THE GIVER-KEEPER GAP

The gap between Christian Givers and Keepers is one of the most significant for church and ministry leaders to negotiate—or, if possible, to close—because it impacts both the "top line" of making devoted disciples and the "bottom line" of meeting the ministry budget.

In the final analysis, it's clear that a "giving soul," revealed by a person's ultimate financial goal, is highly correlated with orthodox beliefs, a personal experience of faith, a premium on generosity as a value and, overall, greater financial contributions. The gap between Givers and Keepers, then, is a soul gap of fruitful discipleship. And the job of ministry is to help people cultivate motives that transcend day-to-day circumstances such that their generous impulses become generous habits, and their generous habits a way of life.

The gap between Christian Givers and Keepers is one of the most significant for church and ministry leaders to negotiate

4. THE STRENGTH GAP

KEY FINDINGS

- People who consider generosity important give more consistently to their church and other ministries.
- People who give more use electronic giving methods more often.
- Individually asking people to give is more effective than asking them as part of a group.

How highly a Christian values generosity tends to correlate with whether, and at what amount, they set aside a regular proportion of income for their local church or another ministry (most churches call this kind of giving a *tithe*). More than half of those who say generosity is *not very* or *not at all* important to them say they do not set aside a certain amount to donate; they either vary the amount they give (30%) or do not give at all (27%). By comparison, nearly two-thirds of those to whom generosity is *extremely* important set their giving at 10 percent of their income (9%), at more than 10 percent (33%) or at a different percentage each year (21%).

Similarly, those who most highly value generosity are six times more likely than those who say it is *not very* or *not at all* important to report donating more than $2,500 during the past year to their church, a ministry or a nonprofit (18% vs. 3%), and three times more likely than those who say generosity is only *somewhat* important (18% vs. 6%). In other words, making giving a priority matters.

EVERY MEMBER SHOULD GIVE SOME AMOUNT TO THEIR CHURCH, BY IMPORTANCE OF GENEROSITY

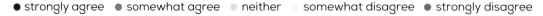
● strongly agree   ● somewhat agree   ● neither   ● somewhat disagree   ● strongly disagree

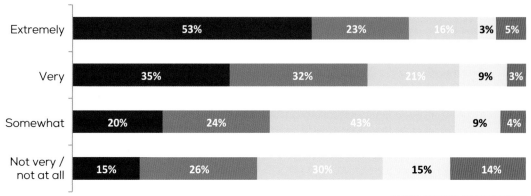

	strongly agree	somewhat agree	neither	somewhat disagree	strongly disagree
Extremely	53%	23%	16%	3%	5%
Very	35%	32%	21%	9%	3%
Somewhat	20%	24%	43%	9%	4%
Not very / not at all	15%	26%	30%	15%	14%

July 2016, n=1,556 U.S. interested Christians.

There are stark differences when it comes to agreement or disagreement with the statement, "Every member should give some amount to their church," with strong agreement much more likely among those who value generosity most.

However, the differences (while still statistically significant) are not as stark when it comes to these folks' expectations for *how much* a Christian should give to their home church. As with the reasons Christians should be generous, examined in chapter 1, there does not seem to be clear consensus on how much Christians should give.

More than three out of four pastors across denominations strongly agree that all members should financially support their church, but there are notable differences between parishioners of different denominations and their pastors. For example, 57 percent of Southern Baptist adults strongly agree (vs. 94% Baptist pastors), compared to one-third of Lutherans (34% vs. 74% Lutheran pastors) and just one-quarter of Methodists (25% vs. 85% Methodist pastors).

> More than 3 out of 4 pastors strongly agree that all members should financially support their church

HOW MUCH CHRISTIANS SHOULD GIVE TO THEIR HOME CHURCH, BY IMPORTANCE OF GENEROSITY

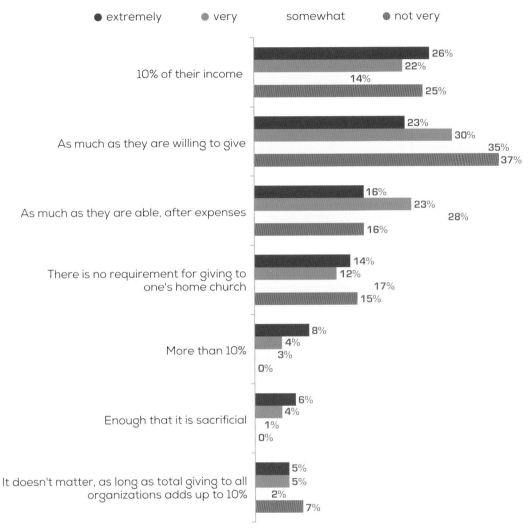

● extremely ● very somewhat ● not very

10% of their income
- 26%
- 22%
- 14%
- 25%

As much as they are willing to give
- 23%
- 30%
- 35%
- 37%

As much as they are able, after expenses
- 16%
- 23%
- 28%
- 16%

There is no requirement for giving to one's home church
- 14%
- 12%
- 17%
- 15%

More than 10%
- 8%
- 4%
- 3%
- 0%

Enough that it is sacrificial
- 6%
- 4%
- 1%
- 0%

It doesn't matter, as long as total giving to all organizations adds up to 10%
- 5%
- 5%
- 2%
- 7%

July 2016, n=1,556 U.S. interested Christians.

ASKING THAT STRENGTHENS GIVING

Barna asked Christians how they responded when asked to give individually or when asked as part of a group, to find out if "the ask" makes a difference to people's giving behaviors. The short answer is yes. Even people who do not consider generosity

"I ALWAYS / USUALLY GIVE" WHEN ASKED INDIVIDUALLY VS. AS PART OF A GROUP, BY IMPORTANCE OF GENEROSITY

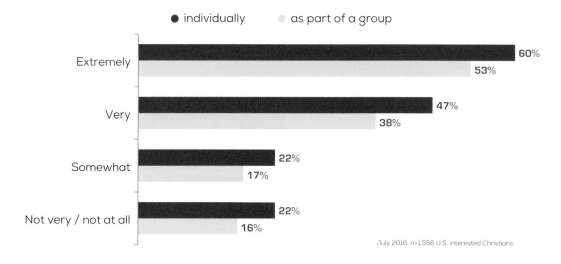

● individually   ○ as part of a group

Extremely	individually	**60%**
	as part of a group	**53%**
Very	individually	**47%**
	as part of a group	**38%**
Somewhat	individually	**22%**
	as part of a group	**17%**
Not very / not at all	individually	**22%**
	as part of a group	**16%**

July 2016. *n*=1,556 U.S. interested Christians.

People's generosity can be strengthened by a face-to-face invitation to give

important are more likely to say "I always give" or "I usually give" when they are asked individually, compared to when they are asked as part of a group.

But many pastors seem reluctant to personally invite people to give. Only one-third says they make a personal, one-on-one appeal twice a month or more often (32%). Those who lead large and growing churches, however, appear to be more comfortable with a personal "ask." Pastors of churches with 250 or more in weekend attendance are more likely to invite someone to give at least twice a month (34%) compared to those with 100 or fewer in attendance (27%). And those who pastor growing churches are more likely than leaders of declining churches to do so (35% vs. 22%).

This is not to say that willingness to individually ask is causal of church size or growth—it's not clear from this study which factors combine to grow attendance. But there is statistical correlation between church size / growth and more frequent personal invitations to give.

Given these findings, it's worth asking if church leaders should branch out from their "offering ask" of the whole congregation to a combination of group and personal appeals. People's generosity can be strengthened by a face-to-face invitation to give.

METHODS THAT STRENGTHEN GIVING

How do people give? Mostly, they put a check (or cash) in the offering plate when it is passed during the worship service. However, a majority of Christians reports their church offers

"I HAVE GIVEN TO MY CHURCH THROUGH ONLINE / WEB GIVING," BY IMPORTANCE OF GENEROSITY & REPORTED ANNUAL GIVING

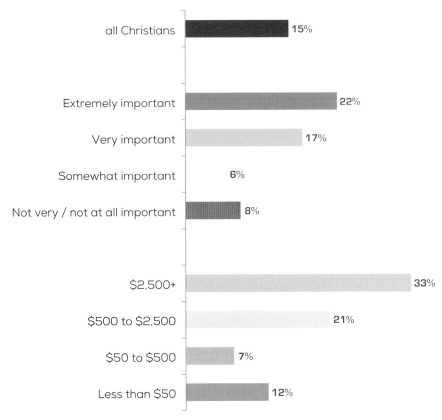

all Christians	15%
Extremely important	22%
Very important	17%
Somewhat important	6%
Not very / not at all important	8%
$2,500+	33%
$500 to $2,500	21%
$50 to $500	7%
Less than $50	12%

July 2016, *n*=1,556 U.S. interested Christians.

electronic giving options of various types—and analysis reveals that those most likely to give do, in fact, utilize these options. For example, 15 percent of all Christians say they have given to their church through online / web giving. But those who consider generosity *extremely* important are much more likely than others to have used this giving method (22%), and those who have donated $2,500 or more are even more likely to have done so (33%). More Givers (motivated by giving goals) than Keepers (motivated by keeping goals) likewise report having donated to their church via online giving.

Another clear finding, which came as a surprise to financial analysts, is that automatic checking account withdrawal (ACH) is massively underused as a method of regular giving; only one-third of pastors report their church offers this giving method (33%). It's possible some parishioners are concerned about incurring fees for their church, but most are probably just not aware that it is an option. (Only 16 percent say their church offers ACH.) One obvious benefit to churches of ACH is consistent weekly offerings independent of attendance; especially during the summer months and holidays, such consistency can make a big difference to a church's cash flow.

What are the takeaways here? Offer electronic giving options in addition to the offering plate or basket. Extend to those most eager (even spontaneously!) to give any and all opportunities to do so. Technology may offer people greater opportunity to flex their giving muscles—including Millennials and younger Gen-Xers, "digital natives" for whom electronic giving is the norm—and many Christians want that chance.

In addition, consider how to connect the dots between automatic or e-giving and compassion. The leeriness some leaders express about electronic methods usually has to do with its potential for set-it-and-forget-it mindlessness. But this potential can be stopped in its tracks with solid teaching paired with opportunities for other, non-financial acts of generosity.

Technology may offer people greater opportunity to flex their giving muscles

LOVE THE LORD YOUR GOD

by David Kinnaman,
President of Barna Group

David Kinnaman is the author of the bestselling books *Good Faith*, *You Lost Me* and *unChristian*. He is president of Barna Group, a leading research and communications company that works with churches, nonprofits and businesses ranging from film studios to financial services. Since 1995, David has directed interviews with nearly one million individuals and overseen hundreds of U.S. and global research studies. He and his wife live in California with their three children.

What is the greatest commandment? According to Jesus, as most Christians know, it is to love God with our whole lives and our neighbors as ourselves (see Mark 12:30). But there are a number of mindsets and heart postures that can sabotage our ability to obey. In this study, our team calls them "gaps."

The findings behind the Mind Gap reveal increasingly divergent expectations between church leaders and Christians (especially Christians under 40) for living generously. The Heart Gap data shows a growing alienation between generations based on their perceptions of each other's generosity (or lack thereof). The differences between Givers and Keepers expose the Soul Gap between selfish and selfless financial goals. And the Strength Gap between people who want to give and their awareness of opportunities to do so show leaders their best bets for connecting generous people with giving options.

Our aim at Barna and Thrivent is not to hand you a menu of ready-made solutions to these very real problems, but to equip you with ways of thinking about the data that can lead you, alongside a broader community of leaders, to answers and ideas that fit your unique ministry circumstances. With that end in mind, let's look at just a few of the challenges posed by each of these gaps and think together about the implications.

GENEROSITY OF MIND

Many churches, and faith-based nonprofits, rely on planned, consistent financial giving—and pastors' tendency to view generosity as "a discipline" or "planned" reflects this reliance. In contrast, more than one-third of Gen-Xers and nearly half of Millennials think of generosity as "spur-of-the-moment," a mindset that appears to be at odds with church leaders' expectations.

It's easy to understand why pastors might be freaked out by this gap. On top of their genuine desire to make disciples who are open-handed and sacrificial stewards of their resources, most pastors have some portion of their family's livelihood at stake: If people don't give, pastors don't get paid.

So the knee-jerk response of some church leaders might be to strategize ways to turn naturally spontaneous givers into planful givers—to close the Mind Gap by trying to change other people's minds. But what if we focus first on our own minds? Is it possible there's nothing inherently wrong with being spontaneously generous, that we're snapping to judgment without considering whether our assumptions can stand up to scrutiny? If we dig into the pages of the Scriptures, might we find numerous examples of disciplined, consistent tithing *and* lavish, spur-of-the-moment generosity? (Hint: Yes.)

Here's something we've consistently found in our research with younger Christians: Millennials are more likely than older believers to appreciate being challenged, to welcome opportunities to rise to the occasion. What a wonderful trait! Why would we want to change it? Instead, let's consider together what it could look like to *respond adaptively* to Christians of any age who are on the lookout for occasions to be generous.

I'm certainly not saying churches should give up on teaching disciplined generosity; the biblical witness and Church tradition emphasize the spiritual benefits of fixed, sacrificial giving practices. But what might you *also* do, in your community and set of

What might you do to invite extravagant, unexpected generosity from people serving an extravagantly generous Lord?

circumstances, to invite extravagant, unexpected generosity from people serving an extravagantly generous Lord?

GENEROSITY OF HEART

I speak and teach hundreds of times a year, and I couldn't tell you how often I listen to sincerely anguished grumbling from older Christians about younger Christians—and vice versa. I'll be honest: I've done it, too. The truth is, generational differences can be difficult to navigate even for those of us whose job is to draw reliable maps.

It's an especially urgent task for Christian leaders who are trying to create and sustain intergenerational community.

One of the main stories we see in *The Generosity Gap* data is the generational divide surrounding generosity—specifically, how the generations ungenerously perceive each other. Older Christians almost uniformly believe that Millennials are, on the whole, lacking in generosity. And when we look at generational differences on what actions are most generous, it's not hard to see why: Young adults tend to prioritize actions that require personal vulnerability and openness to others over financial giving. This priority is neither good nor bad in and of itself, but it is a source of real and dangerous tension in churches.

What can church leaders do to bring unhelpful stereotypes into the open so they don't simmer under the surface? What can you do to help younger and older Christians in your church take themselves lightly and others seriously? How can you challenge people to abandon their preconceived notions in favor of relationships characterized by genuine respect and affectionate generosity?

GENEROSITY OF SOUL

It will come as no surprise to anyone who has read the story of Solomon's early days as a leader that motivations matter. When God offered to grant Solomon anything he asked for, the king didn't ask for wealth, riches or fame but for wisdom to govern his people

> Navigating generational differences is an especially urgent task for Christian leaders who are trying to create and sustain intergenerational community

well. God said to him, "Because your greatest desire is to help your people . . . I will also give you wealth, riches, and fame such as no other king has had before you or will ever have in the future" (2 Chron. 1:11–12). Solomon's ultimate motivation was others-centered, not self-centered—much like the Givers in this study.

That motivations are of ultimate importance is no surprise. Why, then, do we sometimes make them of secondary importance when it comes to generosity? So often we focus our efforts on cultivating generous habits rather than on making generous disciples. Of course, the former is a vitally significant part of the accomplishing the latter; people are less to grow spiritually without concrete disciplines like practicing generosity. But the practices themselves are not the point. The point is who we become under the influence of our habits.

Keeping this front and center may be one key to inspiring habitual giving in those whose first inclination is spontaneity (even as we also offer opportunities to give occasionally and extravagantly!). When focus strays to the discipline itself for its own sake, giving can feel cerebral, dry and lacking passion. But when transformation is the target, generous habits are rightly understood as tools to shape Christlikeness in us. And it's that orientation—toward Jesus—that closes the Soul Gap.

What are some practical ways you can help people major on the major of motivations?

GENEROSITY OF STRENGTH

Chances are good that you have at least one Facebook friend who is into CrossFit®. The first time you scrolled past their list of exercises labeled "WOD," you may have had to Google it ("Workout of the Day"), at which time you discovered an entire CrossFitter vocabulary and swore never again to Google a mysterious abbreviation posted by your phenomenally strong friend.

Maybe that's just me.

Whatever your feelings about CrossFit, churches could benefit from a similar approach to generosity fitness. The objective

> When we attend to the condition of our minds, hearts and souls, the limits of our generosity are stretched and our giving capabilities strengthened

for practitioners of CrossFit is all-around, multi-dimensional strength and conditioning—not jaw-dropping biceps or a four-minute mile, but overall, top-to-bottom, from-the-inside-out fitness that stretches the limits of their physical capabilities.

The chief implication of *The Generosity Gap* data is that the four areas—mind, heart, soul and strength—are deeply interconnected. And that when we attend to the condition of our minds, hearts and souls, the limits of our generosity are stretched and our giving capabilities strengthened.

The place to start, I think, is with a holistic assessment of generosity in your church. How do you communicate about what it is and the many ways to do it? Does your community celebrate those who volunteer *and* those who practice hospitality? Do you hear from people who are generous in different ways, and offer opportunities for generosity in various shapes and sizes (not just the offering plate)?

Perhaps even more importantly, are you thinking and praying together with members of your church family from different generations? My friend Chris Kopka likes to ask, "Are we doing church *to* Millennials or *with* Millennials?" Any internal generosity review your church undertakes must include the input of both younger and older Christians.

Only together can you find an answer to the question, *How can we help each other and our church grow strong?*

AN INVITATION

from Thrivent Financial

Congratulations! The fact that you are now reading this suggests that you've made your way through this entire report and consumed its text, statistics and infographics. Well done!

And yet in life every finish line can also be seen as a starting line. So I'm compelled to ask you, "Now what?" What are your next steps in creating a healthier, more generous church?

As seeds require planting and nurture to bear fruit, ideas require commitment and action to yield results. My hope and prayer is that we don't simply absorb *The Generosity Gap* as information to enlarge our personal trivia collections. So what's a next step worth taking? What is at least one thing you will do to make a positive difference in the lives of the people attending your church as it relates to generosity?

I'm not positioned to answer that question for you, though I do have an invitation for you to consider. If you'd like to join with other church leaders to actively ideate and discuss next steps and best practices connected to the topics in *The Generosity Gap*, I'd love to have you participate in our soon-to-be launched digital community.

Our concept, in a nutshell, is that real church leaders doing real ministry with real people will share ideas and encouragement. For a limited time, you can join the conversation at **InsightWise.org**.

That might be a great next step for you. Or perhaps you'll prayerfully discern a different next step. Whatever paths forward you choose, may God bless you in your work!

Christopher J. Kopka
President, Thrivent Church Solutions Group

Join our community
at **InsightWise.org**

APPENDIX

A. NOTES

1. Morgan Stanley Wealth Management, "Generations Change How Spending Is Trending," MorganStanley.com, August 26, 2016. http://www.morganstanley.com/ideas/millennial-boomer-spending (accessed February 2017).

2. Haver Analytics, Department of Commerce Bureau of Economic Analysis, Morgan Stanley Wealth Management. http://www.morganstanley.com/ideas/millennial-boomer-spending (accessed February 2017).

3. Brian Rashid, "The Rise of the Freelancer Economy," Forbes.com, Jan. 26, 2016. http://www.forbes.com/sites/brianrashid/2016/01/26/the-rise-of-the-freelancer-economy/#5102be63379a (accessed June 2016).

4. Jane Allyn Piliavin and Hong-Wen Charng, "Altruism: A Review of Recent Theory and Research," , vol. 16 (1990), pp. 27–65; Alfred Bandura, "Influence of Models' Reinforcement Contingencies on the Acquisition of Imitative Responses," *Journal of Personality and Social Psychology*, vol. 1 (1965), pp. 589–595; Joan E. Grusec and Erica Redler, "Attribution, Reinforcement and Altruism: A Developmental Analysis," *Developmental Psychology*, vol. 16 (1980), pp. 525–534.

5. U.S. Department of Labor Bureau of Labor Statistics, 2015 National Time Use Survey, "Volunteering in the United States, 2015," February 25, 2016. https://www.bls.gov/news.release/volun.nr0.htm (accessed January 2017).

6. Ibid., Table A–2A, "Time Spent in Primary Activities & Percent of the Population Engaging in Each Activity."

7. Ibid.

8. U.S. Bureau of Economic Analysis, "Real Disposable Personal Income: Per Capita" [A229RX0], retrieved from FRED, Federal Reserve Bank of St. Louis. https://fred.stlouisfed.org/series/A229RX0 (accessed February 2017).

9. U.S. Department of Labor Bureau of Labor Statistics, 2015 National Time Use Survey, "Charts: Volunteer Activities, 2015," December 20, 2016. https://www.bls.gov/TUS/CHARTS/VOLUNTEER.HTM (accessed February 2017).

10. Barna Group, *The State of Pastors: How Today's Faith Leaders Are Navigating Life and Leadership in an Age of Complexity* (Ventura, CA: Barna Group, 2017), pp. 14–15.

11. Barna Group, *The Bible in America: The Changing Landscape of Bible Perceptions and Engagement* (Ventura, CA: Barna Group, 2016), pp. 156–163.

B. METHODOLOGY

The Generosity Gap research consists of data and analysis based on three phases of study. First, in February 2016, Barna conducted 81 qualitative, or open-ended, surveys with U.S. adults ages 18 to 69. These participants were recruited through a national consumer panel that is representative by age, gender, ethnicity, region and socioeconomic level. However, these results are not intended to be representative of, or projected to, the adult population. Also as part of the qualitative phase, 21 Protestant pastors completed open-ended surveys in March 2016 through Barna's PastorPanel. These pastors are broadly distributed across denominations, church size and region, but again, not intended to be nationally representative.

Second, quantitative research was conducted with 1,556 self-identified Christians who have attended church at some point in the past year and who agree, or are neutral, that their faith is very important in their life. These adults represent a range of denominations, including Catholic, mainline and non-mainline Protestant. Participants for this "interested Christians" sample were recruited from a national consumer panel in July and September 2016. The total number of respondents included an oversample of 747 Millennials to enable more robust analysis of this generation, but the *total* sample was then weighted to be representative of the U.S. adult population by age, gender, ethnicity, region and socioeconomic grade. The sampling error on this survey is plus or minus 2.3 percentage points at the 95-percent confidence level.

Third, researchers designed a quantitative survey for U.S. Protestant pastors; 606 completed the survey in June 2016. Participants were recruited through Barna's PastorPanel, publicly available lists and email invitations. Data were minimally weighted to be nationally representative of Protestant churches by denomination, church size and region. The sampling error on the pastor survey is plus or minus 3.9 percentage points at the 95-percent confidence level.

ACKNOWLEDGEMENTS

Barna Group is grateful to Chris Kopka, Jeff Carver, Dave Rustad and the entire Thrivent Church Solutions team for their partnership and missional passion to help churches thrive and Christians to live generously.

The research team for this study is Brooke Hempell, Susan Mettes, Joyce Chiu, David Kinnaman and Aly Hawkins. Under the editorial direction of Roxanne Stone, the writing team for this report is Susan Mettes and Aly Hawkins. The design team is Chaz Russo and Rob Williams. Brenda Usery managed production.

The Generosity Gap team thanks our Barna colleagues Amy Brands, Chrisandra Bolton, Matt Carobini, Inga Dahlstedt, Bill Denzel, Pam Jacob, Jill Kinnaman, Elaine Klautzsch, Steve McBeth, Elise Miller, Josh Pearce, Caitlin Schuman, Todd Sorenson, Sara Tandon and Todd White.

ABOUT THE PROJECT PARTNERS

Barna Group is a research firm dedicated to providing actionable insights on faith and culture, with a particular focus on the Christian church. In its 33-year history, Barna has conducted more than one million interviews in the course of hundreds of studies, and has become a go-to source for organizations that want to better understand a complex and changing world from a faith perspective.

Barna's clients and partners include a broad range of academic institutions, churches, nonprofits and businesses, such as Alpha, the Templeton Foundation, Fuller Seminary, the Bill and Melinda Gates Foundation, Maclellan Foundation, DreamWorks Animation, Focus Features, Habitat for Humanity, The Navigators, NBC-Universal, the ONE Campaign, Paramount Pictures, the Salvation Army, Compassion International, Alpha, Sony Pictures and World Vision. The firm's studies are frequently quoted by major media outlets such as *The Economist*, BBC, CNN, *USA Today*, the *Wall Street Journal*, Fox News, Huffington Post, *The New York Times* and the *Los Angeles Times*.

www.Barna.com

Thrivent Financial is a not-for-profit financial services organization that helps Christians and churches be wise with money and live generously. As a member-owned organization, it offers its members a broad range of products and services, along with guidance from financial representatives nationwide. Thrivent is also dedicated to working with churches to meet their needs for affordable, actionable solutions that support their long-term ministry goals.

Thrivent's approach to connecting faith, finances and generosity has helped strengthen thousands of churches for more than 110 years. Today, Thrivent works with churches to create needed solutions for growth, ideas for engagement and ways to plan for the future. Through these efforts, Thrivent helps strengthen the communities in which its members live, work and worship.

www.Thrivent.com
www.InsightWise.org

Counting the Cost for Church Planters

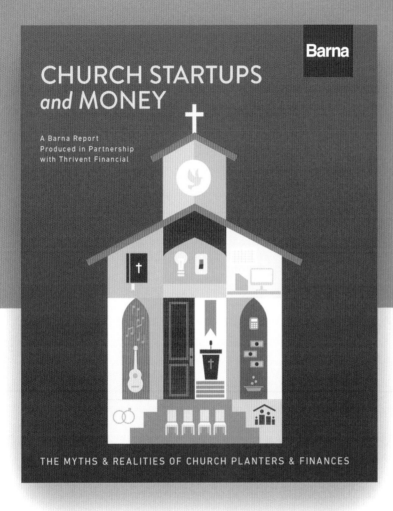

CHURCH STARTUPS *and* MONEY

Barna

A Barna Report
Produced in Partnership
with Thrivent Financial

THE MYTHS & REALITIES OF CHURCH PLANTERS & FINANCES

You will learn

- How church planters perceive their financial situation

- The primary sources of income for planters

- The sources of income that correlate to greater financial stability

- What kind of training and support planters need in order to be effective startup leaders

Church planters are risk-takers who dive headfirst into God's calling to multiply his church. But the financial and administrative challenges of starting a church can take their toll on even the most energetic kingdom entrepreneur.

Produced in partnership with Thrivent Financial, *Church Startups and Money* is a study of the financial realities faced by church planters across the country. Barna interviewed more than 700 leaders whose ministries are in "startup mode" to find out how money—or lack thereof—impacts their ministry, family, and overall well-being. This research provides planters, planting networks, and other stakeholders support to speak honestly about the resources startup leaders need to thrive and plant thriving churches.

Order at
**barna.com
/churchplanting**

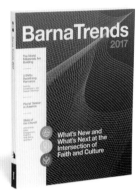
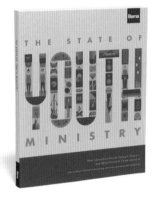
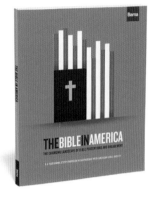
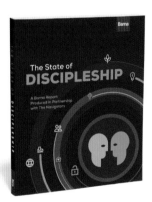
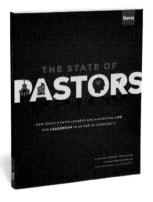